Y0-CYG-815

PAKISTAN
AN ISLAMIC TREASURE

By Jabeen Yusufali

DILLON PRESS, INC.
Minneapolis, Minnesota 55415

Dedicated to Yusuf, Sultana, Yaseen-Ali,
and my parents, Habib and Shirin Jaffer.

Acknowledgments

*Photos have been provided by Anthony R. Dalton; Robin White/Fotolex;
Zia Yusuf; Arthur M. Sackler Gallery/Smithsonian Institution; David Val-
dez/The White House; Fawzia Shivji; S.M. Amin/Aramco World magazine;
Dolores Weiss/Agency for International Development; C. Benjamin/Tom
Stack & Associates; Aliya Asaf; Shahid Zaman; Zahid and Shehnaz Hus-
sain; Hugh McClean Photographic; Sabir Gaya; Pakistan Tourism Development Corporation; and the Embassy of Pakistan.*

Library of Congress Cataloging-in-Publication Data

Yusufali, Jabeen.
    Pakistan : an Islamic treasure / by Jabeen Yusufali.
      p. cm. — (Discovering our heritage)
    Includes bibliographical references.
    Summary: Discusses the history, people, religions, food,
cultural heritage, lifestyle, education, sports, industries, major
cities, politics, historic sites, festivals, and holidays of
Pakistan.
    ISBN 0-87518-433-2 (lib. bdg.) : $12.95
    1. Pakistan—Juvenile literature. [1. Pakistan.]   I. Title.
II. Series.

DS376.9.Y87   1990
954.91—dc20   89-26028
                                          CIP
                                          AC

© 1990 by Dillon Press, Inc. All rights reserved

Dillon Press, Inc., 242 Portland Avenue South
Minneapolis, Minnesota 55415

Printed in the United States of America
1 2 3 4 5 6 7 8 9 10 99 98 97 96 95 94 93 92 91 90

3999901131711

Contents

Fast Facts about Pakistan

Official Name: Islamic Republic of Pakistan

Capital: Islamabad

Location: South-central Asia; Pakistan extends northward from the Arabian Sea for almost 1,000 miles (1,610 kilometers), across the Thar Desert and eastern plains, up to the Himalayan Mountains; Pakistan is bordered on the west by Iran and Afghanistan, on the north by China, and on the east by India

Area: 310,404 square miles (803,943 square kilometers); *Greatest Distances:* north-south—935 miles (1,505 kilometers); east-west—800 miles (1,287 kilometers). *Coastline:* 506 miles (814 kilometers)

Elevation: *Highest*—K-2 mountain, the second highest mountain in the world, at 28,250 feet (8,611 meters) above sea level. *Lowest*—sea level along the coast

Population: 107 million (1988 estimate)

Form of Government: Republic. *Head of Government*—prime minister

Important Products: *Agriculture*—barley, cotton, fruits, rice, sugarcane, tobacco, wheat; *Manufacturing*—cement, chemicals, textiles, fertilizer, leather goods, steel; *Mining*—coal, limestone, natural gas, petroleum

Basic Unit of Money: Pakistani Rupee

Major Languages: Urdu is the official language. Other commonly spoken languages are: Punjabi, Sindhi, Pushtu, and Baluchi

Major Religions: 97 percent Muslim; a small percentage of people are Christians or Hindus

Flag: A white crescent and star on a green background, bordered by a white stripe on the left side

National Anthem: "Paak sar zamin shaad baad" ("Long Live our Pure Land")

Major Holidays: Eid-ul-Fitr (following the Muslim month of Ramadhan); Eid-ul-Azha (month varies according to the Islamic calendar); Independence Day (August 14); Death anniversary of "Quaid-E-Azam," founder of the nation (September 11); Birthday of Quaid-E-Azam (December 25)

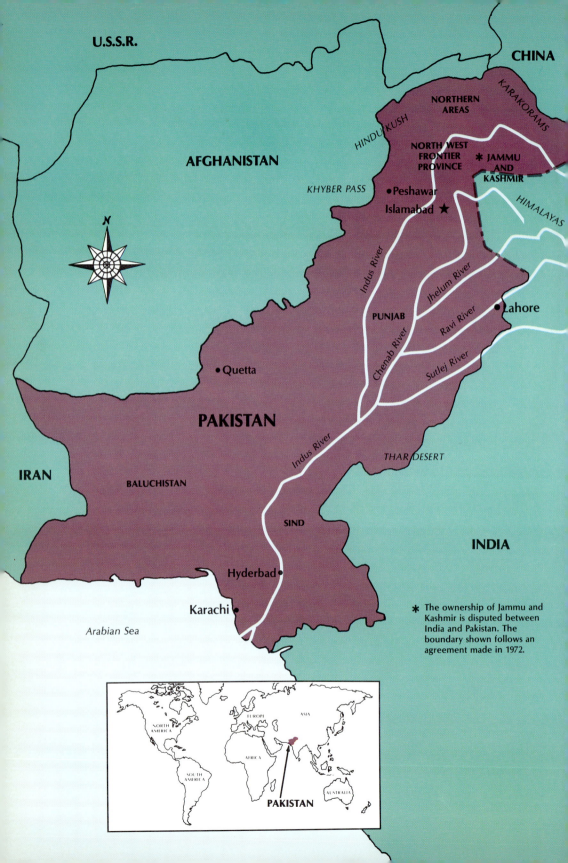

U.S.S.R.

CHINA

AFGHANISTAN

KARAKORAMS

HINDU KUSH

NORTHERN AREAS

NORTH WEST FRONTIER PROVINCE

✳ JAMMU AND KASHMIR

KHYBER PASS

•Peshawar

Islamabad ★

HIMALAYAS

N

Indus River

Jhelum River

PUNJAB

•Lahore

Chenab River

Ravi River

•Quetta

Sutlej River

PAKISTAN

Indus River

THAR DESERT

IRAN

BALUCHISTAN

SIND

INDIA

Hyderbad•

✳ The ownership of Jammu and Kashmir is disputed between India and Pakistan. The boundary shown follows an agreement made in 1972.

Karachi•

Arabian Sea

NORTH AMERICA

EUROPE

ASIA

AFRICA

SOUTH AMERICA

AUSTRALIA

PAKISTAN

1. A Desert Land

For the past five thousand years, the Indus River has nourished the people, animals, and agriculture of the nation now called Pakistan. Flowing through lands high and low, cold and hot, through lush green pastures and dry windy deserts, the Indus River winds its way across the country on its journey to the Arabian Sea.

While people have lived in this area for thousands of years, the country itself is less than forty-five years old. This struggling young nation relies on the Indus River to support its chief industry—agriculture. Receiving a constant supply of water from glaciers in the mountain ranges of northern Pakistan, the Indus rushes southward while its waters are distributed throughout the country by irrigation canals. Without the Indus River, there might not be a Pakistan.

Pakistan is a long, narrow country, about the size of the state of California. It lies in Asia, and forms the western part of the Indian subcontinent. India and Bangladesh, to the east, make up the rest of this large peninsula.

Pakistan stretches northward from the Arabian Sea to some of the tallest mountains in the world. The country has several other neighbors; Afghanistan and

Iran lie to its west, and China and Tibet are farther
north.

In length, Pakistan is almost 1,000 miles (1,610 kilometers) from north to south. It includes deserts, fertile
plains, and three great snow-capped mountain ranges in
the north—the Karakorams, the Himalayas, and Hindu
Kush. Hundreds of mountains ranging 20,000 feet (6,100
meters) and more rise here, including the world's second highest mountain, K-2, which is 28,523 feet (8,617
meters). Some of the world's largest glaciers lie between
these rugged peaks.

Each of Pakistan's four provinces—Punjab, Sind,
North West Frontier Province (NWFP), and Baluchistan—is home to a different cultural group, each with its
own customs and characteristics. The Punjabis, who live
mainly in Punjab, form the largest group. Other important groups are the Sindhis in Sind, the Pushtuns in
NWFP, and the Baluch in Baluchistan. Several smaller
tribes—the Bajaur, Mohmand, Khyber, Orakzai, Kur-
rum, and North and South Waziristan—rule tribal areas
in the north. Some tribes are nomadic and wander
freely across the border into nearby Afghanistan.

The people of each province speak a different language at home—Punjabi, Sindhi, Pushtu, and Baluchi.
Yet in Pakistan, many people speak more than one language. Urdu is the country's official language. English is
also widely spoken. It was brought to this land by the

*Snow-capped mountain ranges rise in the northern areas of
Pakistan.*

British, who ruled the Indian subcontinent, including Pakistan, for almost two hundred years.

Pakistan's different groups share one important characteristic. About 97 percent of Pakistanis follow the religion of Islam. Islam not only unifies the different cultural groups in Pakistan, it guides all aspects of life, government, and business. In a land rich with tradition, history, and natural beauty, this strong faith may be its greatest treasure.

Northern Pakistan

The North West Frontier Province (NWFP) lies close to Afghanistan and China. Here, the three great mountain ranges act as natural borders between the nations. The mountains which separate NWFP from Afghanistan are especially rough and dangerous, and the area is almost barren. The famous Khyber Pass lies in these mountains. Many centuries ago, invaders such as the Aryans, Persians, Greeks, Huns, and Turks entered Pakistan and the Indian subcontinent through this pass. Today, refugees from nearby Afghanistan sometimes try to escape the troubles in their country by crossing this pass into Pakistan.

Peshawar, the capital of NWFP, is only about thirty miles (forty-eight kilometers) from the Khyber Pass. It is an ancient city, rich with landmarks from

Farms cover the hills of Murree, in northern Pakistan.

each wave of invaders. Older districts are crowded with historic forts, tombs, and *mosques*—Islamic places of worship. Newer districts have modern buildings, universities, and research centers.

The southern part of the NWFP is flat and very dry. Toward the southeast, though, there are snow-capped mountains, glaciers, lakes, and lush, green valleys. This area receives a moderate amount of rainfall, which nourishes tall, dense forests. Here, snow leopards, hyenas, musk deer, and wild sheep roam the countryside. The forests and lakes are also home to many different kinds of birds, ducks, geese, and fish.

Islamabad, the capital city of Pakistan, is located in this area. Islamabad is a new city, planned and built from scratch beginning in 1961. New buildings are constantly being constructed in the city, including high-rise apartments, hotels, and one of the world's largest mosques. Most residents of Islamabad work in government offices.

Only twelve miles (twenty kilometers) from Islamabad is a large, historic city, Rawalpindi. The city is a favorite tourist attraction. Its many bazaars, or markets, are crowded with shops and vendors offering gold, silver, brass, copperware, and many colorful handicrafts. The Pakistan Armed Forces have their headquarters in Rawalpindi, and soldiers in khaki uniforms are a common sight.

Many resorts are located in the mountains near these cities. These resorts are especially beautiful during the winter, when many Pakistanis from the southern parts of the country come here to escape the heat. They ski on the snowy slopes and ice-skate on the lakes. Another attraction is the ruins of a famous ancient city, Taxila, located near Rawalpindi. The world's largest salt mine and the world's largest earth-filled dam are also nearby.

To the northwest of NWFP are the Northern Areas, a mountainous region where few people live. Here, the 15,000-foot (4,575-kilometer)-high Karakoram Highway connects Pakistan to China. The highway winds through jagged mountains that are always covered with snow, past the curving Khunjerab River.

Many mountaineers come to this region to climb K-2 and other famous, but dangerous, mountains. One of these is Nanga Parbat, nicknamed the "Killer Mountain." At 26, 660 feet (8,131 meters), it is the third highest mountain in the world.

Baluchistan

While the mountainous areas in the NWFP may be experiencing a snowstorm, Baluchistan could be struck by a desert sandstorm. Most of the southwestern province of Baluchistan is a dry, rocky plateau that is rich in important minerals. Oil, gas, coal, copper, iron ore, limestone, gypsum, and many other minerals are mined here. Natural gas from Baluchistan is transported by pipeline to homes and industries in several Pakistani cities. The world's best onyx, a heavy, marble-like mineral, is mined in Nagundi, a small town in Baluchistan. The onyx is carved into statues, coffee tables, and more.

It is nearly impossible for people to live in the south-western part of Baluchistan. In this hot, rocky plateau, few plants grow because there is hardly any rainfall. But Baluchistan is a land of contrasts. The northern area is cool and filled with juniper tree forests. Almost half of Pakistan's total fresh and dry fruit production comes from this part of Baluchistan. Baluchi farmers also raise a large number of goats, sheep, and other livestock.

There are many lakes and tourist resorts near Quetta, Baluchistan's capital, which lies in the mountains at 5,600 feet (1,708 meters) above sea level. Quetta is a small but busy commercial center surrounded by hills. The city is connected to the rest of the country by air, rail, and road. It is rare to see traffic lights here—most traffic is controlled by traffic police who use hand signals and blow loud whistles.

A large part of Baluchistan borders the Arabian Sea. The sea brings cool breezes and makes fishing an important occupation for many people who live on the coastline.

Sind and Punjab

Southeast of Baluchistan lies the province of Sind. It, too, borders the Arabian Sea. Sind is named after the Indus River, which runs the length of the province and empties into the Arabian Sea near its southernmost

The Indus River flows through Sind Province, providing water for the many farms in the region.

point. Much of Sind is a dry plain formed by soil deposited by the river. A system of canals carries water from the Indus River to farms throughout the plain. This irrigation system has made the Sind plain a fertile agricultural region.

The southeastern part of Sind is a dry, sandy wasteland called the Thar Desert. Few people live there. In May and June, people in many Sindhi cities can feel heat waves and sandstorms blowing in from the Thar

Desert. In the entire Sind province, rainfall is so scarce that when it rains, children go out to play until they are thoroughly soaked.

The dry climate of Sind is ideal for the camel. In Sind's rural and urban areas, it is common to see tall camels pulling heavy carts and moving calmly with the flow of cars and other traffic.

Karachi is the capital of Sind, and Pakistan's largest city and leading industrial center. Located near an excellent harbor on the shores of the Arabian Sea, Karachi is an important port. The city has huge shipbuilding facilities. Gaddani Beach, the world's third largest shipbreaking yard, employs more than fifteen thousand people. The international airport in Karachi is one of the largest in Asia. Seven million Pakistanis from all over the country live in Karachi, making it a very crowded city. People work in the city's steel mills, oil refineries, factories, and automobile assembly plants.

North of Sind is the province of Punjab, a lush agricultural region. Many rivers flow through this fertile area. The Chenab, Sutlej, Jhelum, Beas, and Ravi rivers come together to form the Indus River in Punjab. Water from these rivers is used to irrigate farmland. Punjab's farms are the main suppliers of grain and cotton for the nation.

The majority of Pakistanis live in Punjab. More than three million people live in its capital, Lahore, the

A view of downtown Karachi, with the white dome of the memorial to Pakistan's founder in the background.

nation's second largest city. Once, Mughal kings ruled
the Indian subcontinent from this site. Today, Lahore
has many grand and majestic forts, gardens, mosques,
and tombs built by the luxury-loving Mughals. Tourists
travel to the city to admire these ancient landmarks.

City Life and Village Life

Pakistan's major cities are extremely crowded, yet
more and more Pakistanis move to the cities from the
countryside in search of a job. City people might work
in banks, offices, hospitals, airports, or factories. Many
own their own businesses, ranging from large textile
mills to small newsstands.

In most cities, upper- and middle-class families live
in beautiful houses called "bungalows" or "villas," and in
large apartment buildings. In poorer districts, though,
some families live in two- or three-room mud or cement
huts. Pakistan's cities are very modern in some ways.
People travel in trucks, buses, taxis, and modern rick-
shaws (three-wheeled scooters which carry a driver and
passengers). Yet some traditional ways of life remain.
Goods are still transported by camel, horse, or donkey
carts.

Even though Pakistan's cities are attractive to many
people, about three quarters of all Pakistanis farm for a
living. Life in many rural areas has remained unchanged

Even in cities such as Peshawar, people and goods are often transported by animal carts.

for hundreds of years. Animal carts or bicycles are used for transportation. Many villagers have no electricity or plumbing. Water for drinking and cooking has to be collected from the rivers or public water taps. Cooking is done on coal or kerosene stoves, and clothing is washed at the riverbanks.

In most villages, old farming ways continue. Farmers use ox carts to till the land and manure to fertilize the crops. Very few farmers can afford tractors or

In the village of Dalbandin, a camel driver talks to his camel.

machines to help them on the farm. It is estimated that there are only 25,000 tractors in the country, while 6 million families work on farms!

Usually, though, the farmers' main concern is lack of water. Since rainfall is scarce in many areas, people must irrigate their lands by digging canals at the river-banks, and directing a steady flow of water to their farms. Pakistan has the world's largest irrigation system. The government has constructed many dams on some rivers, which help in two important ways. The dams generate electricity for nearby villages, and they prevent flooding by keeping the flow of river water under control.

Pakistan produces enough of most basic foods to feed its people, and is able to export large quantities of wheat and rice. Tea and edible oil are also produced in Pakistan. But since the supply cannot meet the people's high demand, Pakistan has to import such products to avoid shortages. Pakistan also relies on other countries for petroleum, machinery, electrical goods, chemicals, medicines, and more.

Many countries buy raw cotton, carpets, fish, and other goods from Pakistan. The country is also famous for its handicraft industry. Each province has its own special crafts. Handmade rugs, silk, embroidered textiles, brasswork, and pottery are exported to different parts of the world. These handicrafts, some of which require many hours of human labor, are admired all over the world.

A Democratic Country

Pakistan is a democratic country, where Pakistanis vote for and elect their leaders. But the country has been ruled by martial law more than once in its history.

In Pakistani elections, people in every part of the

Carpet weaving is a Pakistani specialty.

country vote for their choice of representative from the thousands of candidates who run for the 207 seats in the National Assembly. Each province governs itself, similar to the states in the United States. Whichever political party wins the most seats may have its leader appointed as the new prime minister.

The current prime minister of Pakistan is Benazir Bhutto. Her appointment was an important event because she became the world's first woman to lead a

Muslim nation. At the age of thirty-five, she also became one of the youngest heads of government.

In the past forty-five years, Pakistan has created universities, oil refineries, large, busy cities, and one of the largest irrigation systems in the world. While many Pakistanis are poor, the new government is working to improve its people's standard of living. Pakistanis hope that since democracy has been restored, the world will pay more attention to Pakistan and its people.

2. The Pakistani Way of Life

To understand the Pakistani way of life, it is necessary to understand Islam. Because almost all Pakistanis are Muslims, followers of Islam, the religion is an important part of everyday life. In Pakistan, children are taught the basics of Islam when they are very young. Only a few hours after a baby is born, the *azaan*—the words that call a Muslim to prayer—is whispered in its ears. When the child is a few months old, its parents will teach it to hold up one tiny finger and say the words, *Allah eik*, which means that there is only one Allah, as Muslims call God.

Islam teaches its followers that good manners, respect, discipline, and cleanliness are important to human beings. The religion has strict rules that apply to every adult. A Muslim must believe that there is only one God. A good Muslim says prayers every day, gives to people in need, and fasts, or goes without food, for a month every year. Most Muslims try to make a journey, or pilgrimage, to the holy city of Mecca, Saudi Arabia, at least once in their lifetime.

When Pakistani girls and boys are still small, they join their elders in saying *namaaz*, or prayers, five times a day. As they grow older, they learn how to say the

Crowds gather for Juma *prayers outside a Karachi mosque.*

prayers by themselves. At dawn, noon, midday, sunset, and then again right after sunset, the azaan is called from the thousands of mosques all over Pakistan. This call reminds people that it is prayer time. Muslims stop what they are doing and say their prayers, either at home or at the mosque. When they pray, they face in the direction of the holy city of Mecca. Before praying, people wash their faces and hands, and make sure their bodies and clothes are clean. The prayers are not considered acceptable to Allah if a person is wearing clothing that is unclean, stolen, or borrowed without permission.

Juma, or Friday, is an important day for all Muslims because special prayers are held in the mosque on that afternoon. Since Friday is the Muslim day of worship, Pakistan's weekend falls on Thursday and Friday. On Fridays, relatives often gather to enjoy the day and have dinner together. The new week starts on Saturday.

Usually, only men attend the special juma prayers—women say their prayers at home. In general, Pakistani women do not have the same freedom and privileges as women in Western countries. Many of them wear the *purdah*. This Islamic way of dressing covers the entire body, except the face. Some women also wear veils that cover their face, because Islam teaches that a woman should not be seen by any man outside her family. In rural areas, women may spend most of their time at home to avoid contact with men.

At a young age, Pakistani children learn to recognize what is *haraam*—not allowed—and what is *halaal*—allowed in the Islamic religion. For example, alcohol is haraam. No matter what a person's age, drinking of any kind of alcohol is strictly forbidden in Islam.

Muslims are allowed to eat meat from most animals, except pigs. Yet meat can be eaten only if the words, "In the name of Allah," have been said by the butcher who slaughtered the animal. If the meal on the

A young Pakistani wears a dupatta, *a long scarf most Pakistani women use to cover their heads.*

table has not been prepared according to these rules, it is haraam and should not be eaten. Muslims are also forbidden to lie, steal, cheat, or charge interest on borrowed money.

Remembering Allah

Pakistanis who believe in Islam know that it is their responsibility to choose between right and wrong. The *Koran*, also spelled *Qura'an*, is the holy book that Muslims use as a guide for living.

Muslims believe that only Allah can cause events to happen. Through their prayers, they ask him to protect and guide them, and to help keep them on the correct path. They also repeat certain phrases to remind themselves of the power of Allah. *Bismillah* and *inshaallah* are everyday Arabic words that are spoken by Pakistanis many times during the day.

Bismillah is a short way of saying *Bismillahi-r-rahmaani-r-raheem*. This phrase means, "I begin in the name of Allah, the most compassionate and merciful." Muslims use this phrase before beginning any simple action, such as eating a meal.

Inshaallah means simply, "If Allah wills." Muslims say this to remind themselves that only Allah can control what happens. They use it when talking about events in the future. If a young person asks a friend to play after school, the friend may say, "Inshaallah, after I finish my homework!"

When Pakistanis meet, instead of saying "Hi" or "Hello," they say, *"Assalaamo Alaikum."* This means, "May Allah bestow peace upon you." The person who hears this must return the same greeting. When asked how she is, the person usually responds by saying she is fine. Then she adds, *"Al-hamdu-lillah,"* which means "by the grace of Allah." In Pakistan, people say these words frequently, remembering Allah and expressing gratitude to Him for whatever they are blessed with.

A Resourceful People

Pakistanis earn the highest salaries on the subcontinent. But compared to people's earnings in many other countries, this is still a very low amount. Only a small percentage of Pakistanis are rich enough to be able to afford expensive homes, cars, refrigerators, air conditioners, or telephones.

Because they do not have much of their own, most Pakistanis value their few possessions highly. If something breaks, they always try to find a way to fix it. No matter how old a car, radio, or typewriter may be, they attempt to repair it.

People who cannot afford new things can buy used goods. Many second-hand shops sell old, but good, items over and over again. For example, some school textbooks remain in use for decades. For what would cost less than a dollar, book-binding companies can repair old, tattered books. With new hard covers and strongly bound pages, the book gets a new life. Such books are passed down from student to student for many years and can be resold many times.

Some Pakistanis even earn a living by repairing and recycling used goods. The *dabble-wallah*, or box-man, goes from house to house collecting used goods for recycling. He gathers old newspapers, tin cans, boxes, and bottles, and even pays the family for the goods he collects.

Pakistani Entertainment

Most Pakistani families do not spend much money on entertainment. In the evenings, families may go for a drive, sit on the balcony and talk, or watch television. The government owns and operates Pakistan's five main television stations. It produces many high-quality local programs, but comedies, detective stories, and movies from England and the United States are also shown. The national news is broadcast in Urdu, English, Arabic, and regional languages. Television is relatively new to Pakistan. The first broadcasts took place in 1968, and color television has only been recently introduced.

Many Pakistanis enjoy watching movies. Theaters in the cities show movies made in England, the United States, and Pakistan. Because Islam forbids men and women to kiss or show affection before marriage, the scenes that show people kissing are always cut out of foreign movies. Pakistani censors also cut out scenes in which actors wear revealing clothes, because that would offend most Muslims.

Pakistan's own moviemaking industry is a giant enterprise. Every year it produces large numbers of movies in the Urdu, Punjabi, or Sindhi languages.

These movies are quite dramatic, with complicated plots similar to those in American soap operas. Songs are used to help express the sad, happy, or troubled feelings of the hero or heroine. Pakistani audiences enjoy watching movies with fights, car chases, and fierce-looking villains. Many moviegoers take their films very seriously. Actors who play villains are sometimes beaten up by people who confuse them with the characters they play.

In addition to sports and movies, art and poetry are popular in Pakistan. Several times a year, groups of Pakistanis arrange meetings where both famous and beginning poets recite their works. These are sometimes broadcast on radio and television. Another favorite form of entertainment is a *ghazal*. This is a slow, poetic song accompanied by sitar, violin, and *tabla* (a type of drum) music. There are many ghazal singers in Pakistan. New, contemporary artists are encouraged, too. Some like to sing songs set to Western-style music with guitars, drums, and electronic keyboards.

Most Pakistanis appreciate the different types of folk music that come from the various parts of Pakistan, even if they do not understand the words in a song. Folk musicians wear their regional folk dresses and play instruments from their area. Local festivals and television stations feature both unknown and well-known folk singers from different cities and even remote villages.

Although Pakistan is made up of a large variety of tribes and peoples, the Islamic faith binds Pakistanis together. Modern Pakistanis are eager for progress, but still treasure their traditional music and stories. Above all else, they value their religion.

3. A Young Nation, An Ancient History

Although Pakistan is a young nation, it has an ancient history. As part of the Indian subcontinent, Pakistan shares a history with its neighbor, India, that dates back almost five thousand years.

The earliest residents of the Indian subcontinent belonged to one of the oldest civilizations in the world. These ancient people lived in the cities of Moenjodaro and Harappa and other smaller towns along the Indus River. Today, this area is part of the Sind and Punjab provinces of Pakistan. Scientists believe that this civilization began more than four thousand years ago. The people of this time planned their towns carefully and built them in an orderly manner. Buildings were constructed of baked brick, and many even had bathrooms.

The Indus River civilization had disappeared by about 1700 B.C. Scientists do not know why this huge civilization ended. Many believe that the people may have been destroyed or driven away by a great plague, a massive flood, or invaders from another land.

Invaders from across the Mountains

Over the centuries, the Indian subcontinent has

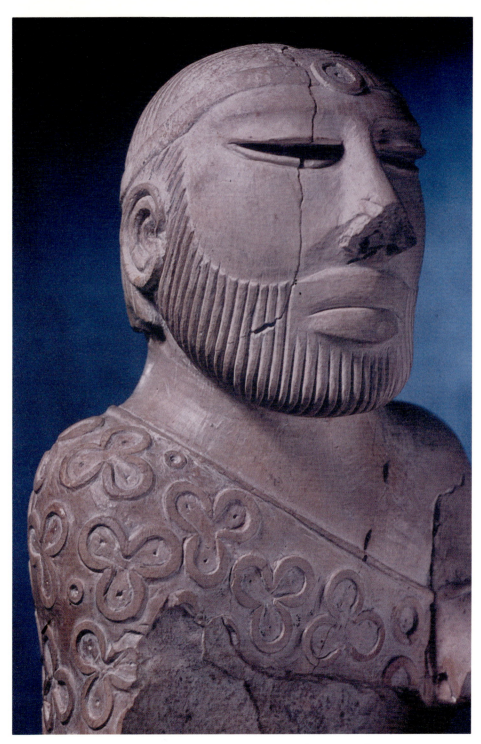

An ancient sculpture of a King Priest of Moenjodaro.

been invaded many times by many different groups of people. The earliest invaders were large bands of Aryan nomads. Around 1500 B.C., the Aryans migrated into the Indian subcontinent through passes in the northern Hindu Kush mountains. These tall, fair-skinned people arrived with their families, their sheep, and their cattle. India was already home to a dark-skinned people, the Dravidians. But the warlike Aryans soon forced the Dravidians to be their slaves, causing some to flee southward down the Indian peninsula. Over time, the two races mixed, and new generations produced people of fair, dark, or medium complexions.

The Aryans brought the Sanskrit language and the Hindu religion to the subcontinent. During the sixth century B.C., the Buddhist religion was founded in India. It was spread across the subcontinent during the Maurya Empire, the first great empire to rule most of the subcontinent.

Invaders continued to move across the subcontinent through the mountain passes in northern Pakistan. At various times, the land where Pakistan is today was conquered by armies from Persia (now Iran), Greece, Afghanistan, and other Asian lands. Pakistan became part of two great Indian empires, the Kushan Empire and the Gupta Empire.

In the eighth century A.D., Arab Muslims invaded Sind, bringing the Islamic religion to the subcontinent.

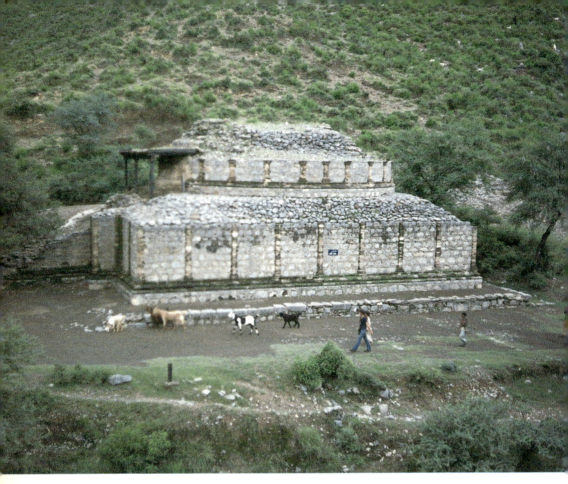

An archaeological site at Taxila, once a Buddhist center of learning.

Many people converted to the new religion from Hinduism and Buddhism. Waves of Muslim invaders followed, including Turkish Muslims around the year 1000.

In 1525, a descendant of the famous Mongol, Genghis Khan, invaded Pakistan and India from nearby Afghanistan. This man was a fierce warrior named Babur. Babur founded the Mughal dynasty, a family of powerful, wealthy Muslim kings. The Mughals ruled the entire Indian subcontinent for the next two centuries.

The Mughal Empire

Fierce as he was, Babur also appreciated beauty. He built many magnificent gardens throughout his empire. His descendants inherited his love of beauty and built majestic forts, palaces, mosques, and tombs across the subcontinent. Many of these impressive structures are still standing in Pakistan today, especially in the city of Lahore.

The Mughal kings lived a life of luxury. They encouraged the arts, music, and literature, and loved jewelry, expensive clothes, and richly prepared foods. The Mughals introduced Urdu, a language related to Arabic and Persian, to their empire.

The early Mughal kings were powerful and wise rulers, and Babur's grandson, Akbar, was one of the greatest. When Akbar became king, he was only thirteen years old. For forty-nine years, he ruled his empire wisely. Akbar attempted to teach his people to live in harmony, whether they were Hindus or Muslims, of fair or dark complexion.

For centuries before Akbar's reign, the peoples of the Indian subcontinent had fought with each other. There were large groups of Hindus and Muslims. Since Hinduism and Islam are very different religions, the two groups rarely agreed. While Muslims believe in one god, Allah, the Hindus believe in many gods. While Muslims

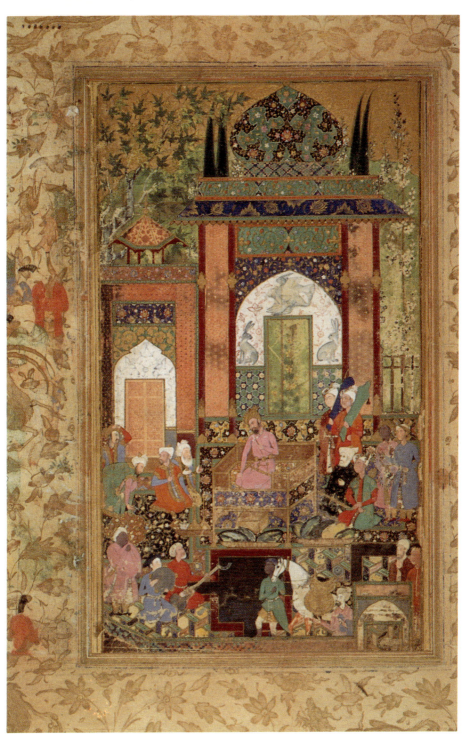

This painting shows Babur, the first great Mughal king, in his court.

eat beef, Hindus do not because the cow is a sacred animal to them. Akbar decided to treat everyone equally, teaching his people to live together with respect for each other's beliefs.

The British *Raj*

In 1601, British traders came to the Indian subcontinent in large numbers. They soon took control of the land with their company, the British East India Company. The company had offices in several cities and was protected by small armies. England started to profit from its trade with India.

The last Mughal king to have strong powers was Aurangzeb, who ruled India from 1658 to 1707. Aurangzeb was very strict and sometimes cruel. He caused many Hindus to rebel against him. When Aurangzeb died at the age of ninety-two, the Mughal empire started to weaken. Instead of one strong central government, the land became divided into small kingdoms. Each of these was ruled by a prince, or *rajah*. The rajahs of these kingdoms started fighting terrible wars against each other.

The British government saw this as an opportunity to conquer and rule the Indian subcontinent. In exchange for trade and loyalty, it offered small kingdoms British weapons and protection. The British encouraged the kingdoms to wage war against each other. Aurangzeb's son, Bahadur Shah Zafar, still ruled parts of India at this time, but with little power. The British government finally took control of the subcontinent, including present-day Pakistan, in 1858.

England profited from its *raj*, or rule, in India and stayed for almost two hundred years. The British built roads and railways, established post offices and a telephone system, and provided better hospitals. Schools and universities were made available to the people, English was introduced to the country, and a few Indians were even able to study in England. While many advances were made on the subcontinent, the people began to grow restless under British control. They wanted to rule their country themselves. This bitter struggle for freedom would last many years and cost thousands of lives.

The first rebellion against the British was started by a group of Muslim soldiers in the British army. These soldiers were supplied with grease-coated cartridges for their new rifles. A rumor broke out that this grease was pig fat. To the Muslims, contact with any pig-related product is forbidden, and they refused to touch the cartridges. Riots broke out, and many people were killed.

For almost a year, the Muslims fought many battles against the British. They were always defeated, however, because the small kingdoms stayed faithful to the British, offering armies and support. Finally, the Mughal dynasty ended when Bahadur Shah Zafar was arrested and banished from India.

Two Nations

In the early twentieth century, some educated Indians began voicing their opinions in government affairs. In 1885, a group called the India National Congress was formed. It demanded more participation in Indian politics. Mohandas Gandhi and Jawaharlal Nehru, two Indian Hindus who had been educated in the West, became prominent political activists. Mohammed Ali Jinnah, a Muslim lawyer who had also been educated in the West, joined Nehru and Gandhi in the fight to obtain rights for Indians. Later, however, Jinnah came to believe that the India National Congress was mostly interested in the rights of Hindus. He and Sir Syed Ahmed Khan, an Indian Muslim, formed the All India Muslim League in 1906. Both the India National Congress and the All India Muslim League had the same goal—self-rule for India. The parties failed to agree, though, on a method of government that would allow both Hindus and Muslims equal rights.

Tension built up until both parties demanded that the British leave India for good and grant them complete freedom to govern their country. At this point, the people of India were split into two groups, Hindus and Muslims. The deeply felt, centuries-old problem of religious differences had reached a serious stage.

Realizing that the conflicts between the two religious groups were impossible to settle, a well-known Muslim poet and philosopher, Dr. Mohammed Iqbal, came up with an idea. He suggested that the parts of India which were occupied mostly by Muslims be formed into an independent nation. A list of such provinces was made. The name "Pakistan" was created by putting together *P* for Punjab, *A* for the Afghans in the Northern Areas, *K* for Kashmir, *S* for Sind, and *istan*, the Urdu word for "land of." In Urdu, Pakistan also means "Land of the Pure." In 1940, Mohammed Ali Jinnah made a speech announcing the plan to divide India, which was known as the Pakistan Resolution.

Bloody riots broke out all over the country when people heard of the idea of separating India into two countries. Small arguments erupted into terrible clashes. Thousands of people were killed because of religious differences. After centuries of living together, it now seemed that the people had completely lost their respect for each other.

The British recognized that India was on the verge of a civil war. They decided to leave India and grant the country complete independence. Mohammed Ali Jinnah insisted that it was necessary to form the state of Pakistan before they left. Finally, the British agreed to this demand and began working out a plan to partition, or divide, India.

The India National Congress objected to the areas the Muslim League wanted as Pakistan. To simplify the division, the ruler of each provincial area in question was asked whether he wanted to join India or Pakistan. To the disappointment of many Muslims, India was allowed to keep Kashmir—whose people were 85 percent Muslim—because its *maharajah* (king) was Hindu and wanted to join India.

The Partition

Pakistan was officially founded on August 14, 1947. The new nation consisted of two pieces of land nearly one thousand miles apart, with India in the middle. The larger piece, West Pakistan, consisted of half of Punjab, the whole of Sind, Baluchistan, and the North West Frontier Province. The other piece, East Pakistan, was a part of the province of Bengal, which was mostly inhabited by Muslims. Jinnah knew that this distance would make governing the new nation difficult, but he had no choice.

The partition was a difficult period for every Indian and Pakistani. The biggest population transfer in the history of the world began. Six million Muslims left

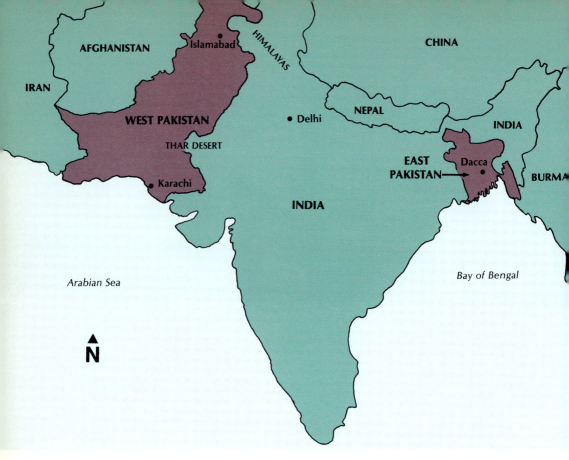

This map shows India, East Pakistan, and West Pakistan after the partition.

India, traveling to Pakistan on foot and by animal cart. Millions of Hindus and Sikhs from Pakistan began migrating to India in the same way. Thousands of refugees were killed when the people of different religions clashed while fleeing past each other toward opposite boundaries.

It is thought that the struggle for independence cost both countries a quarter of a million lives. This was just the beginning of more difficult times to come—especially for Pakistan, which had to create a completely new nation.

Mohammed Ali Jinnah, founder of Pakistan.

Pakistan on its Own

Mohammed Ali Jinnah became the first governor general of Pakistan. Today, Pakistanis refer to him as *Quaid-e-Azam*, the "Founder of the Nation." His picture is lovingly displayed in many Pakistani homes. Jinnah had led millions of people to freedom, but he now faced the difficult responsibility of establishing Pakistan as a country.

In the partition, Pakistan was given 20 percent of the Indian government's movable property. This included furniture, machinery, library books and equipment, and a part of the army. This transfer of goods caused many arguments and sometimes divisions between the two countries were made in a ridiculous way. There were cases of encyclopedia sets being split, dictionaries being halved, and decisions being made by the toss of a coin! As expected, there were many items that could not be divided.

Governing Pakistan was another problem for the new country's leaders. New Delhi had been India's capital, and remained India's capital after the partition. All important files and documents were still kept there. Also, when new government officials were appointed in Pakistan, there were no offices from which to work. Many officials had to work from tents. Pakistan had no telephone, no telegraph, and no railway or bus service. Indian currency was stamped with the word *Pakistan* to create temporary money. Soon after Pakistan's first year as an independent nation, Jinnah died of tuberculosis. He had not had time to solve his country's many problems.

From the beginning, there were many conflicts in Pakistan's government. Liaquat Ali Khan, the nation's young prime minister, was assassinated in 1951 soon after he took office. For many years after, cabinet officials were replaced almost constantly, creating an unstable government. In 1958, to bring the government under control, martial law was imposed by President Iskander Mirza and his young commander in chief, General Ayub Khan. In 1962, General Ayub became president and he ended martial law.

In September 1965, war broke out between Pakistan and India over a promise that India had made in 1948 at the United Nations. Since partition, many small fights had occurred in Kashmir. Indians and Pakistanis still both claimed that region as their own. The United Nations had offered to monitor a "plebiscite," which meant that the Kashmiri people would vote to choose between India and Pakistan. India had agreed to this, but later proved unwilling to go ahead with its promise. Many soldiers were killed in this war, and many became prisoners of war. The United Nations eventually managed to quiet relations between the two countries, but the problem remains unresolved. The areas of Jammu and Kashmir are still marked "disputed territory" on world maps, and border fights still occur.

The Loss of East Pakistan

In 1969, General Ayub was forced to resign. General Yahya Khan, commander in chief of the army, became president, and imposed martial law again. Yahya

Khan scheduled elections for December 1970. By this time, however, the East Pakistanis were beginning to feel left out of important political and economic decisions. They revolted against the Pakistani government, demanding self-government and independence from West Pakistan. They wanted their own land, called Bangladesh, or "Land of the Bengalis." Many East Pakistanis migrated to India when the revolution began, seeking refuge from the fighting.

When Yahya Khan sent Pakistani armies to East Pakistan, the Indian government sent its own armies to help the East Pakistanis defend themselves. Soon, a war between West Pakistan and India broke out. India won the war, and East Pakistan was renamed Bangladesh.

More Martial Law

With the end of the 1971 war, President Yahya Khan was forced to resign, and Zulfiqar Ali Bhutto took over as prime minister of Pakistan. Bhutto ruled the country until 1977, when he was overthrown by General Mohammed Zia Ul Haq. Again, martial law was imposed on Pakistan—the third time since independence. President Zia was a harsh ruler, and allowed no political activity among the people for many years. Bhutto, the former prime minister, was arrested and hanged in 1979. For many years, his family was kept under house arrest, then exiled from Pakistan.

President Zia promised to lift martial law and allow Pakistan to become a democratic nation. Many years passed, however, before Zia announced the end of martial law. Meanwhile, the Pakistani and Indian governments worked to establish a commission to improve relations between the two countries. The commission is meant to promote cooperation in trade, cultural activities, and other areas.

In December 1985, President Zia legalized political parties and rallies, and restored much of the constitution. An election date was set for 1988. The political parties in the country began rallying. One of the candidates was Benazir Bhutto, who had returned to the country from exile in 1986. The former prime minister's daughter was the leader of the Pakistan People's Party, and a favorite among Pakistanis. Huge crowds greeted her wherever she went.

In August 1988, President Zia was killed in a plane crash. The elections were held as planned, however, and Benazir Bhutto was elected prime minister of Pakistan. Bhutto's victory surprised many people. In most Muslim nations, women do not have the same rights as men. Benazir's father, though, had been a popular leader, and Benazir Bhutto had been educated in Western schools, such as Oxford in Great Britain. This made her very different from the majority of Pakistani women.

Prime Minister Benazir Bhutto meets with U.S. President George Bush in Washington, D.C.

One of Prime Minister Bhutto's goals as leader of her country is to improve the standard of living of Pakistanis. Pakistani women were especially glad when Bhutto was elected. They felt they would now be treated more fairly than they had in the past. While Bhutto has had little success in changing many of the current laws, she continues to try.

Pakistan has had a troubled beginning as an independent country. Today, many Pakistani children are able to listen to their country's entire history from the very first Pakistanis, who are now grandparents or great-grandparents. Both the old and the new generations hope for a progressive and peaceful future for their nation.

4. Legends, Superstitions, and Beliefs

In the old, twisting bazaars of Peshawar, there is a famous street called *Qissa Khawani*, which means the "Street of Storytellers." In the past, there were no newspapers, radios, or televisions. Newcomers to the city would come to this bazaar and relate stories about their adventures. These tales were repeated by storytellers and passed down from generation to generation. For hours, as was the tradition, people would sit around a *hookah*, a long pipe filled with water and tobacco. They smoked the hookah in turns, and their puffs made bubbling sounds in the long pipe as they listened to story after story.

Today, people still enjoy gathering on Qissa Khawani. They spend many hours in cafes, discussing past and present events while sipping cups of hot tea.

Love and Tragedy

When the sun sets in Pakistan, mothers tuck their children into bed and tell them stories, often about the man on the moon. They might also sing lullabies which ask *chanda mama*, the "uncle on the moon," to help the children sleep. The children feel safe, believing that angels and fairies will be sitting by their beds all night, watching over them and helping them have happy dreams. When the children are older, they like to hear fairy tales. However, some Pakistani fairy tales do not have happy endings!

One such tale tells of the *naagans*. According to legend, if a man sees a beautiful maiden in the woods or by a lake, she may be a fairy, or naagan. If the man is wise, he will avoid contact with her. Although nagaans appear to be beautiful maidens, they are really from a clan of snakes, taking the human form at will. Falling in love with a naagan is always hopeless, the legend says, and has terrible results. One or both of the lovers will die, because such maidens must marry within their naagan clans.

Many Pakistani legends tell of doomed lovers who come from separate tribes. In most of Pakistan's tribal areas today, people are expected to marry within their own tribe. The parents or older members of the tribe choose the marriage partners and, out of respect, young people rarely disobey their elders. In a typical story, a young village maiden falls in love with a passing stranger while collecting water from the lake. The innocent maiden ignores the old saying, that strangers are unfaithful lovers who will make false promises. The stranger declares his love for the maiden, but then leaves the village and never returns. In other versions, the stranger

A mural depicting different Pakistani legends.

may return after a very long time has passed—only to find that his love has just committed suicide.

One famous Punjabi folktale tells the story of a young girl, Sohni, who fell in love with Mahiwal, a man from a rival tribe across the Chenab River. The lovers realized that if their relationship was discovered, the villagers would beat Mahiwal to death and put Sohni's family to shame. So the two met secretly under dangerous circumstances. At midnight, Sohni would float across the river with the help of an earthenware pot. After a short meeting with Mahiwal, she would float back to the village in the same way. One night, unknown to Sohni, her brother's wife spied on her. Since her family could not lay hands on Mahiwal, they secretly replaced the earthenware pot with a cracked one. That night, Sohni slowly and quietly drowned in the river because the leaking pot could not keep her afloat any longer. When Mahiwal tried to save her, he, too, drowned.

Legends of the Great Mughals

Pakistanis tell many stories about the Mughal era. The powerful Mughal rulers lived in luxury while they ruled the subcontinent for two centuries. Their vaults had so many treasures that they were counted by weight—pounds of gold, silver, and gems, including

A painting from the Mughal era.

pearls, emeralds, coral, jade, and topaz. Other treasures included a large number of jewel-studded daggers and mirrors, and golden and silver jeweled thrones. To ensure that kings and young princes always had good luck, treasures were sometimes measured against their weight on a huge scale and were given away as charity.

At times, though, the Mughals could be quite cruel. Sometimes, brother killed brother in order to be king. Eight of the twenty-seven Mughal kings reigned for less than a year before being murdered by the next heir to the throne.

One of Pakistan's saddest legends is about Anarkali, a dancer in King Akbar's court. The Mughal king became furious when he learned that his son, Prince Salim, had fallen in love with Anarkali. To stop his son from marrying the commoner, Akbar ordered that Anarkali be put to death. Her only crime was that her beautiful smile had charmed the prince. Anarkali was made to stand in one spot while the king's men worked for hours, laying bricks around her and burying her alive. Anarkali sang haunting farewell songs to her love until the last brick was in place and she could be heard no more.

Akbar died after forty-nine years of rule and left the Mughal empire extremely wealthy. When Prince Salim became king, he was known as *Jehangir* (King of the Worlds). At the age of thirty-six, he became the world's richest and most powerful monarch.

Jehangir heard stories about a woman who was said to be the most beautiful in the land. He was told that she was a brave hunter who could kill four tigers with five arrows. Jehangir decided to kill her husband and marry her himself. After the husband's death, he made the woman his queen. She was given the title *Nurjehan* (Light of the World) because Jehangir loved her very much. He found his wife to be confident and wise, and he often consulted her about daily affairs. Some stories even suggest that she became the main decision-maker in the kingdom.

Jehangir prided himself on the way he maintained justice in his kingdom, ordering an "eye for an eye, a tooth for a tooth." But one day, he had to make a decision about punishing the queen.

Armed with a bow and arrow, Queen Nurjehan had been hunting for deer from one of the towers of the Lahore Fort. When she saw a tiny movement far away in the bushes, she fired her arrow. Tragically, she killed a *dhobi*, a man who laundered clothes for a living. The poor man's wife came to Jehangir and tearfully told him that the queen had made her a widow. Without batting an eye, Jehangir said, "Then you have the right to make Queen Nurjehan a widow, too." The poor woman could not follow this ruling and kill the king. She bowed her head and simply left the court.

Superstitions and Beliefs

Pakistani stories usually have a moral to them. Pakistani superstitions and sayings, too, are designed to teach the listener something.

Morals are often taught to children through witty sayings. "Heaven is found at the feet of a mother" teaches children to always respect and serve their parents, for this love will earn them a place in heaven. There is a popular superstition that acts as a reminder for children to help around the house, just in case they have forgotten the saying. If a child sees a shoe facing upside down, that child's mother will face certain death.

Another folk belief probably started as a means to protect oneself from an enemy. Many Pakistanis will never hand a knife or pair of scissors directly to another person. Instead, the object will be passed by setting it down and allowing the other person to pick it up. Passing a sharp object may mean a future argument and a "cut" in friendship.

The Western proverb, "patience has its virtue," is similar to the Pakistan saying, "The fruits of labor are sweet." The saying, "behind every needle follows a thread," reminds children that every action has its consequences.

To Pakistanis, the most important sayings are the *Hadith*, a collection of sayings by the Prophet

Mohammed. Mohammed founded the Islamic religion in the seventh century. Sayings in the Hadith may be only two or three lines long, but they deliver many rules of behavior and messages for living suggested by the Prophet for all Muslims. One example is, "A person who acts without knowledge is likely to do more harm than good."

As taught by Islam, Pakistanis believe that earthquakes, floods, and other events in nature mean the nearness of the Day of Judgement. For example, when an eclipse is predicted, the streets are almost deserted during the event. People rush home and stay indoors, refusing to watch the eclipse. In their homes, people lay out their prayer mats and prepare to offer special prayers to Allah.

A strong belief in the wisdom of Allah is just one part of the Pakistani heritage. Through many stories and sayings, Pakistan's children are taught the ways of their ancestors and pride in their young country.

5. Festivals and Special Events

In Pakistan, the sighting of a new moon is an important event because it indicates that a new month of the Islamic calendar has begun. Muslims follow a lunar calendar, in which each month begins with a new moon. Similar to the calendar followed in the Western world, the lunar calendar has twelve months. Yet each month is only twenty-nine or thirty days long, and the Muslim year is about ten days shorter than the year on the Western calendar.

A Month of Hardship

The ninth month of the Muslim calendar, *Ramadhan*, is eagerly awaited by all Pakistanis. Muslims believe that, during Ramadhan, the doors of heaven are thrown open and Allah is especially forgiving. Daily life in Pakistan changes in this special month. Days are quieter than usual. Schools close at midday, people in offices and factories work shorter hours, and shopkeepers close their shops early. Everyone tries to rest or take an afternoon nap whenever possible.

The reason for this change is that Muslims are required to fast during the whole month of Ramadhan.

Only very young children, pregnant women, and sick or elderly people do not have to fast. From dawn until sunset, Muslims who fast cannot eat food or drink liquids. People may eat and drink before the sun rises and after it sets, but not during daylight hours. An hour or two before dawn, windows in Pakistani homes start lighting up as people wake up to have a small snack. Fasting starts when the first rays of the sun are seen.

By fasting, Muslims feel that they can understand the suffering of the poor and less fortunate people of the world. Fasting is considered healthy and good for people because it helps them develop self-discipline. Since Ramadhan is seen as the holiest of all months, Muslims spend most of their time praying to Allah and reciting the Koran. People make a special effort to be as truthful, peaceful, tolerant, generous, and religious as possible so that their fasts are acceptable to God. Those who fast try to keep from complaining about hunger and thirst. Pakistanis who are not fasting for any reason do not eat or drink in public.

Young children are eager to prove their ability to fast. At first, parents let them fast for a few hours. Later, the children fast for half a day. When a child is considered old enough to endure thirst and hunger, parents allow him or her to keep the first full fast. Parents encourage their fasting children to save their energy and take long naps. A child's first full fast is an important event. After it is completed, the child is showered with congratulations and gifts from family, neighbors, and friends.

Each day during Ramadhan, a siren sounds at sunset. The call to prayer is announced from the minarets, or tall towers, of the mosques. These sounds signal that it is time to end the fast. Because it is not possible for a person to eat a big meal immediately after fasting all day, the Pakistani people eat at leisure. After a fast, it is important to drink a lot of liquids, too, to restore water that the body has lost during the day.

Pakistani mothers and wives make an extra effort to prepare a variety of delicious foods and desserts for the evening meal. At home, people invite friends and relatives to join them for *iftaar*, as this breaking of the fast is called. On the streets, small groups of men gather to eat a picnic-like iftaar, sitting on blankets or on patches of grass. Street vendors sell an assortment of fried snacks for people to eat. Strangers who have not been able to make it home for iftaar may be invited to join these picnics, since people should not delay breaking their fasts.

An hour or so after iftaar, Pakistani cities seem to come alive. Streets are lit with neon shop signs and street lights. People flock to the bazaars to purchase new clothes, shoes, jewelry, glass bracelets, fruit, meat, and sweets for the big celebration expected at the end of the

Bazaars and marketplaces become crowded during the final days of Ramadhan.

month of Ramadhan. Although restaurants close their drapes during the daytime, at night they offer all kinds of treats and fruit juices to the busy shoppers.

Pakistan's bazaars and shopping centers are especially busy during the last few days of Ramadhan as people prepare for the upcoming holiday. At post offices, long lines of people wait to mail their holiday greeting cards. Airports and bus and train stations are crowded with people journeying to family reunions.

Eid-ul-Fitr

On the night of the twenty-eighth fast, Muslims of all ages start searching for the new moon in the starlit sky, and begin preparing for the coming *Eid*, or festive holiday. When the sighting of the moon is officially announced, they know that Ramadhan is over. The next day will be *Eid-ul-Fitr*, a feast that celebrates the end of the month of fasting. The news is quickly spread by radio, television, and telephone. Many people make a quick trip to the bazaar for last-minute shopping or to the tailors to pick up new clothes for the family. Children apply *mehndi* (a reddish-black paste made of crushed henna leaves, cloves, and black tea) on the palms of their hands. The dye becomes crusty when it dries, so mothers carefully put an old sock on the child's hand before bedtime.

The detailed mehndi *designs can take hours to apply.*

Eid-ul-Fitr is much like Christmas in the Western world. Housewives clean the house and unpack the best linen and dinnerware for the Eid feast. On the holiday morning, the members of the family rise early, bathe, and dress in their new clothes. The women dress in elaborately embroidered outfits and gold jewelry with many glass bracelets.

Adults take time to admire the pretty, reddish henna patterns on their children's hands. Then the family

During Eid celebrations, children may spend their money on balloons and other toys.

has a special breakfast of sweet vermicelli—a type of pasta—cooked in milk, with saffron, dried fruits, and nuts. The men and boys gather in the mosque or a nearby park, where they will offer special Eid prayers. Together, following one leader, thousands of men pray to Allah, rising, bending, and bowing at the same time. After that, the men embrace and greet each other with the phrase, *Eid Mubarak*, which means "Eid greetings." Before returning home, they usually go to the cemetery to say special prayers for dead friends and relatives.

All day, families visit each other, hug, and say, "Eid Mubarak." Plates of cakes, pastries, and sweetmeats are exchanged between neighbors, relatives, and friends.

On this day, children greet adults by kissing the back of the adult's right hand, after first touching it to each eye. The children receive gifts of money from their parents, grandparents, and aunts. At the end of the day, children happily count their money to see how much they have collected. The Eid celebration will continue for two more days, and the children may spend part of their money at the circus, zoo, or amusement park.

Eid-ul-Azha

About two months after Eid-ul-Fitr, another Eid will take place. *Eid-ul-Azha*, the feast of the Sacrifice, is celebrated on the tenth day of the last Islamic month. Although most Pakistanis celebrate this Eid at home, each year a large number journey to Saudi Arabia, to celebrate in Islam's holy city of Mecca. Many of these people will have saved all their lives to make the pilgrimage, or journey, which is called *Hajj*. Muslims believe that when they make this pilgrimage, they are cleansed of all sins.

A few weeks before Eid-ul-Azha, the Pakistani

Islam's holy city of Mecca.

men, women, and children who are making the Hajj board ships and planes bound for Jeddah, Saudi Arabia. From Jeddah, they will drive to Mecca. People who make this long pilgrimage are considered very fortunate and are greatly respected. When Pakistanis say good-bye to their Mecca-bound relatives and friends, they ask to be remembered in prayers. The farewell event is usually an emotional occasion, mixed with laughter and tears, even though the pilgrims will return in about two weeks.

Eid-ul-Azha is held in memory of the occasion when the Prophet Ibrahim was about to sacrifice his son Ismail, according to God's instructions. As the prophet was about to begin the sacrifice, Allah showed his pleasure at Ibrahim's obedience by replacing the boy with a sheep, sparing Ismail's life. On this Eid, Pakistanis attend prayer services in the morning and celebrate for two or three days with more prayers and huge feasts with lots of meat. People may sacrifice a sheep, goat, cow, or camel in memory of the Prophet Ibrahim. The meat is distributed to poor people, friends, and relatives. To meet the high demand for meat, shepherds bring flocks of fattened sheep and goats to the big cities, hoping to make their best deals of the year. The sheep's wool is dyed bright pink, green, or blue, adding much color to the busy cities!

Soon after Eid-ul-Azha, the pilgrims start returning from Mecca. All of Pakistan's airports are crowded with people welcoming the *Hajjis* (titles given to people who have performed Hajj). Pilgrim women clip off a small strand of hair before they return, but the men usually shave off all their hair.

In the following days, before the Muslim year ends, Hajjis are frequently invited to dinner in the homes of different relatives and friends. The conversation will be mostly about the journey to Mecca that every Muslim wishes to make at least once in his or her lifetime.

More Celebrations

The new Islamic year begins on a sad note. During the first days of the first month, *Muhurram*, several million Pakistani Muslims wear black and mourn the death of Imam Husain, grandson of the Prophet Mohammed. For these ten days, the Pakistanis attend special services at mosques and residences, and mourn while the story of Husain's death is retold.

On *Ashura*, the tenth day, huge processions wind through streets and villages. Small stalls are built on the street curbs, offering free sherbet, sweetened fruit juice, or chilled water to thirsty marchers.

A couple of months later, Pakistanis throughout the country celebrate *Eid-Milad-un-Nabi*, the birthday of the Prophet Mohammed. Social gatherings are held where poets read poems in praise of the Prophet. Others sing *kasidas*, poems that honor the Prophet. All over the country, schools plan stage programs where children sing kasidas. The special Eid program is attended by families of the schoolchildren, and everyone wears their best clothes to the event.

Christmas is celebrated in Pakistan by more than

750,000 Pakistani Christians. They go to church and attend many parties during the holiday. Many other people offer prayers at the tomb of Mohammed Ali Jinnah, the founder of Pakistan, because he was also born on December 25. Others spend the holiday by having a picnic, relaxing at the beach, or just enjoying a quiet day at home.

All of Pakistan's provinces celebrate several agricultural folk festivals each year. During March, several festivals are held in the Punjab province. One is a six-day event called the *Awami Mela*, or People's Festival. People gather to watch sporting events, cattle displays, and animal acrobatics. Folk artists of all ages come from remote villages to sing and give dance performances.

In Peshawar, the Pathans and Afghans of the North West Frontier Province gather to celebrate an annual folk festival in April. Tribal people in colorful costumes sing and perform traditional dances. Sometimes teams of men on horses divide themselves into two teams to play polo or a rough and dangerous game called *chapandoz*. In this game, horsemen pick up the headless body of a goat from the ground at one end of the field, race it around a marker at the opposite end of the field, then return to drop the goat at the starting point. If a rider falls off his horse, he could be trampled to death by the other horses.

Pakistani festivals and holidays are usually celebrated together as a family. The religious celebrations are special because they bring together families, neighbors, and friends. Any feuds between people are put aside as they meet to celebrate their Islamic and national heritage.

6. The Pakistani Family

Pakistani families are usually very close-knit and spend a lot of time together. This closeness helps them communicate and get along with each other better. Because of this, very few marriages in Pakistan ever end in divorce.

Most Pakistanis are part of an extended family in which grandparents, parents, children, and grandchildren all live together in the same house. Pakistani children become very close to their grandparents because they spend a lot of time with them. If a child's parents are busy, a grandmother will find the time to talk with or make a special snack for the grandchild. When a child is sick, a grandparent may stay up all night to care for him or her. Many widowed grandmothers share the same bedroom with the younger children. These children may cuddle up with their grandmother to hear a story, or to find some sympathy when their parents have been upset with them.

Physically as well as emotionally, Pakistani children stay close to their parents and grandparents. Young women are usually the only people who leave home when they become adults. When women marry, they move in with their husband and his family.

Pakistani young people spend a great deal of time with their parents.

Families and Islam

Pakistani families are usually large because children are considered to be a favor from Allah. Teaching children religion is one of the most important functions of family life. Parents try to spend as much time as possible with their sons and daughters, guiding them in the right way to live. Spending time together and going out as a family seems natural to most Pakistanis. Children accompany their parents to almost all social events—festivals, weddings, and even dinner parties.

Parents spend much of their lives raising children. This teaches the children that later, when their parents are older, it will be their turn to look after them. There are no such things as nursing homes in Pakistan, mostly because elderly people live with their married children. These elders try to be as helpful as they can and also take care of the grandchildren. That way, families stay close together and are always there for each other in times of need.

The Islamic religion plays another important part in everyday life for young people. Because Islam does not allow men and women to meet alone before marriage, dating is not allowed in Pakistan. For this reason, most Pakistani marriages are arranged marriages—parents choose a suitable partner for their children.

The process begins when the two families exchange photographs of the young people in question, and check the backgrounds of the family members. If both sets of parents think the match is suitable, they arrange a meeting for the boy and girl. The couple does not meet alone, but is able to chat at a small tea party with their parents present. Afterward, if the boy and girl agree, the wedding is arranged.

A Pakistani couple on their wedding day.

Pakistani weddings can last from two to five days. Guests are usually invited as whole families. If party rooms or hotels cannot be used, a road near the bride's or groom's house may be blocked off and a huge tent erected on it. Chairs, dinner tables, decorations, and lights are installed. The tent is divided so that men and women can sit and dine in separate sections.

A day or two before the wedding, friends apply mehndi to the bride's hands and feet in beautiful designs. The mehndi is washed off the next morning, revealing a bright red pattern that will last for weeks.

On the day of the wedding, a *qazi*, a religious scholar or priest, receives the bride's consent privately and then recites the *nikah*, or wedding vows. Finally, the couple's very first private meeting takes place after all the guests have eaten and gone home.

A happy event such as a girl leaving home to get married is also a sad, tearful event for her and her family. From the time she is a child, though, a girl's parents think of her as a very special guest whose permanent home is with her future husband's family.

A Love of Entertaining

Pakistani people often invite guests over for meals. Each important event in a family member's life is celebrated with relatives and friends.

When a baby is born, word of the happy event spreads fast. Within one or two days, relatives and friends visit the mother and child with gifts. When a baby is seven days old, the family holds an *aqeeqa* ceremony, in which the baby's hair is shaved off. Wealthy families weigh the baby's hair against gold, and a sum of money equal to the price of this gold is given to the poor. Traditionally, a goat is sacrificed, and a feast is held after the aqeeqa.

When the child is six years old, the family holds a *Bismillah* ceremony. Relatives and close friends are invited to take part. The child is taught to recite the Arabic alphabet, his or her first lesson in learning to recite the Koran. For many months, the child will learn the basic rules only, and then will be able to start reading from the actual book. When the child has read all thirty chapters of the Koran, the parents will once again invite relatives and friends to join them in celebrating.

Home Sweet Home

Pakistani homes and apartments in the cities are usually big, with several large rooms. Most, though, have only one bathroom. Well-to-do Pakistani families may live in attractive bungalows and may own cars and television sets. They usually hire servants, gardeners, and perhaps even chauffers.

A village in northern Pakistan.

Middle-class families live in smaller houses or apartment buildings. Some apartment buildings are quite tall, but none of them have elevators. If a child forgets something, he usually shouts up to his *ammi*, or mother. The forgotten item will be tossed to him from the balcony or lowered down in a basket tied to a string!

Poor people in Pakistan live in huts made of bricks

and mud with thatched roofs. These are usually located in areas outside the city boundaries. Most Pakistani villages have this type of housing as well.

Most of the poor sleep on a *charpie*—a wooden bed using woven, knotted ropes as a mattress. Only a few villagers can afford to buy cotton or sponge mattresses. Most villagers own little or no furniture. At mealtime, a cloth is spread on the clean kitchen floor, and families sit cross-legged around it to eat their meals.

Well-to-do Pakistanis in the cities live a modern life similar in some ways to wealthy people in Western countries. In many ways, though, it is quite different. For example, it is rare for a Pakistani family to own a dishwasher, washing machine, air conditioner, or a microwave oven.

Household Help

Being a homemaker in Pakistan is not a simple task since most housework is done without the help of modern appliances. Because of this, almost all upper- and middle-class families hire one or more servants to help at home. Servants do the laundry, wash the dishes, and sweep and mop floors.

Starting at dawn, city buses are crowded as the helpers start commuting to one or more homes they work in. Helpers may come in for a couple of hours each day to mop floors or dust, or shop for groceries for the day.

Since few Pakistanis can afford refrigerators, most food must be purchased fresh every day. During the day, vendors roll heavy, produce-filled carts down the streets, calling out the name of what they are selling. The housewife can call a vendor to her door and select her purchase if she does not have a helper.

Children and Chores

Because children in poor families work very hard to help support the family, many do not go to school. Children may be involved in the family farming or fishing business, employed as carpet weavers, or apprenticed with a carpenter, tailor, or other tradesperson. Some young people clean cars in parking lots, or shine shoes on sidewalks. Girls usually stay home to help cook, clean, and take care of younger brothers and sisters.

The children of middle- and upper-class families rarely do any housework. Instead, they spend their time studying or playing. When a girl reaches her teenage years, she will help her mother in the kitchen. A Pakistani girl is expected to learn the art of cooking at an early age. After a meal, the women of the family begin clearing the table, sometimes with the help of servants.

Though women are free to work, very few middle-

This young boy works as a servant in a Karachi home.

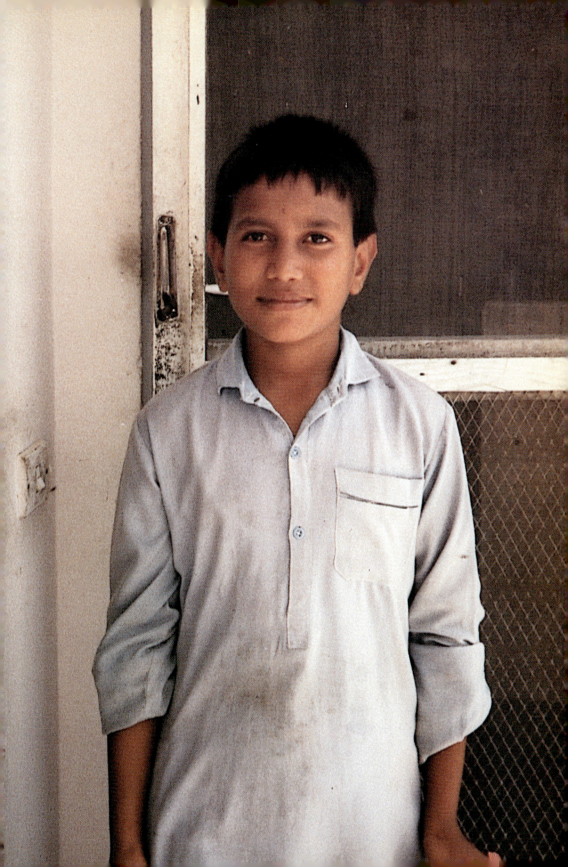

or upper-class Pakistani women pursue careers. Most women, even those educated in good schools, stay home after marriage because of family tradition. Most Pakistani husbands believe that if the mother is home, the family will receive better care. When children return home from school, their mother or one of their grandparents is usually home.

The Pakistani father is considered the head of the family, and rarely helps with housework. Young boys, too, are not expected to do chores around the house.

The Pakistani Kitchen

Pakistani food is prepared using clarified, or liquid, butter and fragrant spices. Cinnamon, cardamom, cloves, black mustard seeds, coriander, saffron, and other spices are commonly used in everyday cooking. Since most Pakistanis prefer their food hot and spicy, hot, crunchy green peppers are often served with a meal.

Pakistani housewives use deep aluminum pots for cooking rice and curry, a spicy dish seasoned with curry powder. Frying is done in a round pot that looks like a wok.

Most work in a Pakistani kitchen is done by hand. Before vegetables are cooked, they must be soaked so that any soil may sink to the bottom of the pot. Rice is cleaned handful by handful, so that no dirt particles or

In most Pakistani villages, people shop at outdoor spice markets.

stones end up in the cooking pot. Even flour must be sifted before it is used. Although many supermarkets have been built in Pakistan's larger cities, very few foods in the country are available frozen or canned.

In Pakistan, the main meal of the day is usually lunch. After lunch, many people rest at home for a couple of hours before returning to work. Later in the afternoon, they may have tea with a snack. Dinner is served shortly after sunset. It is usually a lighter meal than lunch. In the late evenings, many Pakistani families sit on their balconies or in their courtyards, under the open sky. They may sit for hours, snacking, sipping tea, and talking.

A Pakistani meal usually consists of curry made with meat, fish, or vegetables, along with a flat, round wheat bread called *chappatti*, or *roti*. Rice may also be served instead of rotis. Some families buy hot *tandoor* rotis from restaurants where they are made fresh all day long. The *tandoor* oven is a deep, red-hot clay oven that is built a few feet underground. The temperature in this oven is extremely high—several hundred degrees higher than in a conventional oven. Pakistanis especially like rotis made in a tandoor oven. They also enjoy *tandoori chicken*, chicken that is soaked in tamarind juices and broiled in the tandoor.

With care, you can make tandoor rotis in your oven broiler at home. You may wish to ask an adult to help you with this recipe.

Tandoor Rotis

2-1/2 cups white flour
1 cup warm water
1 teaspoon salt
1 packet dry yeast
3 tablespoons oil
butter

In a large bowl, mix together all the ingredients except the butter. You may not need all the water. Use only enough to make the dough smooth and elastic, not sticky. Knead the dough well. Cover the bowl with a roomy dish, and let the dough rise in a warm place for 1-1/2 to 2 hours.

Turn your oven setting to "broil." After the dough has risen, punch it down and divide it into six balls. Dust a handful of flour on a flat surface, and use a rolling pin to roll each ball into a round, flat shape about six to eight inches in diameter. Try to make the thickness even.

On the stove, heat a heavy skillet on medium-high heat. Place the roti on the skillet for one minute. Do not flip the roti over. With a long-handled spoon or spatula, remove the roti from the skillet and place it under the broiler. Within seconds, it will puff up. Remove it as soon as the roti turns brown. Spread butter on the roti and serve it immediately. Serves 6.

Kheema Mattar Curry

1 pound ground beef
1 teaspoon salt
1 clove crushed garlic (or 1 teaspoon garlic powder)
1/2 teaspoon crushed ginger

1 cup diced onions
1 cup diced tomato
1 medium potato, diced
1 cup green peas
1/4 cup oil
1 cup water
1 teaspoon curry powder
1/2 teaspoon lemon juice
1/4 cup fresh, chopped coriander (cilantro) leaves

In a deep skillet, sauté the onions in oil until they are golden brown. Lower the heat and add the garlic, ginger, and curry powder. Stir for one minute, then add the chopped tomato. Sauté for another minute, then add ground beef and salt.

When the ground beef has browned, add the water, peas, and potato slices. Mix well. Cover and let simmer until potatoes have cooked somewhat soft, about 10 to 15 minutes.

Add the lemon juice and coriander leaves just before serving with the tandoor rotis. Serves 6.

Pakistanis, like Americans, serve some special foods on holidays. One of these is a sweet vermicelli dish known as *sheer khorma vermicelli*. This dish is also sometimes eaten as a dessert, and is a favorite among Pakistani young people. Pakistanis use a particular kind

of vermicelli, known as "Rolex" brand vermicelli. In the
United States, this may be available at Asian grocery
stores, and even in the pasta section of some larger
supermarkets. If you are not able to find the wheat vermicelli, you may substitute angel hair pasta, a very thin,
spaghetti-like pasta.

Sheer Khorma Vermicelli

1/4 pound Rolex brand wheat vermicelli (or angel
   hair pasta broken into short strands)
3-4 cups whole milk
1 12-ounce can condensed milk
1/2 cup sugar (or more, to taste)
2 teaspoons freshly ground cardamom
1/8 teapoon saffron
1 tablespoon uncooked rice
1/2 teaspoon vanilla
1/2 cup chopped almonds and pistachios

Soak the rice in water for one hour. It is best not to
use instant rice. Remove the rice from water and
crush in a blender to sugar-sized particles. Set aside.

Over very low heat, cook the whole milk, condensed milk, and sugar for 1-1/2 hours. Stir occasionally to keep the milk from burning. The mixture will thicken slightly and change color.

Add the saffron, cardamom, and rice. Cook for 15 to 30 minutes, stirring occasionally, until the rice particles have softened.

Add the vermicelli (or angel hair). Cook for 15 minutes, stirring from the bottom of the pan to keep the vermicelli from sticking. Add the vanilla, almonds, and pistachios. Stir slightly and spoon into bowls. Serves 4.

Here is another simple, sweet dish you can try.

Shahi Tukra

6 slices of white bread
butter
1/2 can sweet condensed milk
1 cup whole milk
orange food coloring
1/8 teaspoon saffron
sliced almonds and pistachios

Trim the crust from the bread, and cut each slice into four squares. Heat a frying pan and fry both sides of each square in butter. Combine the milk portions, food coloring, and saffron. Stir these ingredients, and heat the mixture slowly until it is consistent and has a fragrant aroma. Soak each square in this mixture and arrange carefully on a plate. Sprinkle sliced almonds and pistachios thickly over the Shahi Tukras. Pour remaining milk mixture over them. Serve the Shahi Tukras warm or at room temperature. Serves 4.

7. *A Thirst for Education*

When Pakistan was first founded, most of its people could not read or write. Until that time, most schools on the Indian subcontinent were British. The Muslims—who later became Pakistanis—would often not attend these schools because they resented British control.

After the partition of India and Pakistan, the new Pakistani government began building schools, colleges, and universities in Pakistan. As new roads were built into some of the remote tribal areas, schools and colleges were established there, too. Within thirty-eight years, the country created more than 86,000 primary, middle, and high schools. It also created almost 900 arts, science, and professional colleges, and 20 general and professional universities. The Open University of Islamabad contributes to educating Pakistanis, too. It offers classes through radio, television, and correspondence courses.

In remote areas, the government has established more than eight thousand "mosque schools" to teach basic elementary schooling. In cities, many Pakistani students attend private Christian schools, regardless of what faith they follow, because their parents think private schools provide a better education. There are also

The Institute of Medical Sciences in Islamabad.

vocational schools available to the millions of Pakistanis who want to learn a trade as soon as they graduate from high school. In this way, they can immediately start helping to support their families.

Learning to Read

Although the Pakistani government thinks education is important, the majority of the country's people

do not. Only 26 percent of adults can read. More than
75 percent of Pakistanis are farmers. These families find
it difficult to allow their children to attend school, even
though primary schooling is free. In the countryside,
young children are needed at home to care for babies
and do the housework, allowing parents and older children to work in the fields. In poor homes, girls, especially, receive little or no schooling. Their parents believe
education will be of no use to them, as they are expected to marry and become homemakers someday. In
the cities, poor children are expected to find jobs as
carpet weavers or in other occupations to help their
families survive.

In past years, however, more and more parents in
rural areas have begun to realize how important it is for
their children to receive a good education. They may
save money for much of their lives to send their children
to school. These parents may never learn to read themselves, but they believe their children will have a better
life someday because of the education they receive. Still,
many young people drop out of school after only five
years.

Children in Pakistan are not required to attend
school. Instead, the government uses other ways to encourage education. Cash awards and scholarships are
provided to help needy families cope while their children
attend school. The government sets aside more funds

each year to provide such scholarships and to build larger, more efficient school systems in each province.

At School

Children of most middle- and upper-class families in towns and cities attend school. Their parents have usually received some education themselves, and they give their children much encouragement. Since hired helpers are available to do the chores around the home, this gives schoolchildren time for classes and homework.

Many children walk to school. Small children and young girls are sometimes escorted to and from school by a nanny. Other children commute to school by public bus. On public buses, women and small children can only occupy a small area near the driver. About three quarters of the bus is occupied by men.

Traveling to school by bus can be difficult because most buses are overcrowded. Schoolchildren will try to squeeze onto an overcrowded bus because they fear they will be late to school if they wait for the next one.

Many schools provide privately owned or rented buses, but they may charge a monthly fee to the parents. Compared to the cost of the public bus, this charge can seem expensive. Children from wealthier families have a comfortable ride to school in a car driven by one of their parents or a chauffeur.

Most schools require a uniform. Boys wear pants or shirts, the color of which depends on the school they attend. Girls wear *shalwar* (loose pants), *kamiz* (a long dress), and a shawl called a *dupatta*, which covers the bosom and hangs over the back of both shoulders. Girls usually wear their hair in one or two long braids.

At school, the very small boys and girls sit together in one classroom. When they get older, though, boys and girls attend separate classes. Most Pakistani schools and colleges are either all male or all female. Usually, men teach the boys, and women teach the girls.

When a teacher first enters the classroom, all the students rise and say, *"Salaam Alaikum"* ("Peace be upon you"). Teachers are treated with great respect and are never called by their first names. Instead, they are referred to as "Miss" or "Sir." Sometimes, one teacher will teach all the subjects of the day, and at other times, different teachers teach different subjects.

Most Pakistani schoolchildren in villages do not use textbooks. Instead, teachers read from textbooks and write the information on the blackboard. Students copy the work in their blank notebooks. Printed worksheets are rarely used in either villages or cities, because of the high cost of printing such materials.

At school, children learn Urdu, English, and perhaps a local language. They will also study Islamic history and the basics of Islamic religion. Other subjects

A group of young boys in their school uniforms.

include civics, home economics, math, history, science, geography, and physical education.

Entrance Exams

When girls and boys enter the tenth grade, they must pass the Secondary School Certificate (S.S.C.) examination. They will then be able to enter college.

The board of education of each province prepares

the examinations for the area. During April or May, students are told which school they will go to for their exam. Each student is assigned an identification number called a "roll number" which will be used instead of their name throughout the week-long exam.

The test papers arrive in the classroom sealed. All supervisors open them at the same time and hand them out to the waiting students. The students are warned not to write their names anywhere; the papers are graded according to their roll numbers. After the exams, the papers are collected and sent to the board of education for grading.

Because the millions of papers are corrected and graded by hand, the students must wait all summer for their results. It can be a very anxious time for them. While they wait for the scores, parents and students must decide which college the son or daughter will attend during the next school year. There are three types of colleges to choose from—liberal arts, science, and commerce—according to the type of career a student is interested in. A Pakistani interested in becoming a teacher, for example, would choose to attend an arts college.

There is a lot of excitement in Pakistan the day the S.S.C. examination results are announced. Newspapers carry pages and pages of the printed roll numbers, announcing the scores in order of total points. If a student

In recent years, more women have begun to attend Pakistan's universities.

does not find his or her number there, it means that he or she has failed one or more of the subjects on the test. The examination in the failing subject or subjects must be taken again during "Supplementary Exams." These are held later in the year for all students who did not pass the first test. The students who passed the S.S.C. are congratulated by family and friends, and the proud parents send plates of sweetmeats to neighbors and friends.

Many teenagers are finished with schooling after their S.S.C. exams. Students who want to continue their studies attend college and take the Higher School Certificate (H.S.C.) examination. This test is held two years after the S.S.C. exams.

College and university education depends not only on the students, but also on the financial status of the family. In Pakistan, where most unskilled work is taken by poor people to help feed their families, students do not have many chances to find part-time jobs to help pay for tuition. Most young people drop out of college because their parents cannot afford a university education, which is very expensive. As Pakistan's cities grow, however, more jobs are created. Many students now have the chance to help pay their way through college.

Pakistan and its people have changed much in the past decades. Today's students can attend a law school, engineering school, agricultural school, or even a university specializing in nuclear science without ever leaving Pakistan.

Thousands of young Pakistanis are becoming teachers, lawyers, doctors, dentists, engineers, airplane pilots, and scientists. Many go abroad to specialize further in their field. As they graduate, get jobs, and go into business for themselves, these young women and men are helping Pakistan develop into a stronger nation.

8. Sports in Pakistan

When Pakistani children return home from school, their day is not quite over yet. Most children look forward to the moment when they can go and play with their friends. After having a snack, doing their homework, and spending at least half an hour with an Islamic tutor, the children are free to play outside until dusk.

Because the Islamic religion requires that young men and women not spend time with each other before marriage, young boys and girls in Pakistan rarely play together outside school. Young girls usually like to play "house" with their dolls, and many girls even marry their doll to their best friend's doll. The small guests arrive at the "wedding party" in their best outfits, and with their best dolls in tow. Sometimes, girls also play in a park, supervised by an adult. But as girls grow older, they do not usually play outside the house. Instead, older girls learn creative skills such as embroidery, calligraphy, and other crafts. In the cities, many girls attend classes to learn sewing or painting, while others take foreign language classes or international cooking classes.

Young boys spend much of their free time outside the house, playing tag, running, or flying homemade kites. Kite-flying can be a lot of fun with a group of

In a sewing class, Pakistani women and girls make clothing for an upcoming Eid celebration.

Pakistani boys. Crushed glass is glued to the kite strings, and the boys then try to have fights in the sky. The battle between the two kites may last for hours. When a severed kite is seen floating down from the city, friends cry *"Wo-katta"* ("Cut")! Then they run all over the neighborhood trying to catch the kite. If the kite gets stuck in a tree, the first boy who climbs and retrieves it is the new owner of the kite.

Another favorite pastime among boys is riding bikes. In fact, some curious young men take their bicycles apart to understand how they work.

School Sports Day

There are not many community centers in Pakistan where children can exercise, play games, or swim. Since the few centers or clubs are quite expensive, only the children of well-to-do families belong to such organizations. The one opportunity that most Pakistani children have for special sports is at school. A special sports day is held by schools during March each year and is quite an important event.

Each school has three main sports teams, called "houses," which compete against each other for ribbons, prizes, and trophies. The team that comes out as the winning house is awarded a trophy or plaque by the chief guest. This is an invited guest who is usually an important political figure in the area.

The house captains start preparing for the sports day months in advance. The best athletes train hard, and there is a lot of excitement as the children practice for the different events. Among them are high jumping, gunnysack racing, relay racing, and volleyball.

On the afternoon of the annual sports day, the school playing field is decorated with brightly colored tents called *shamianas*. The tents flutter in the breeze and give shade to hundreds of visitors—parents, friends, and children. In the back of the playground, stalls serve cold drinks and snacks during breaks.

The athletes stand at attention on the field as they await the arrival of the chief guest. The school band plays the Pakistani National Anthem, and hundreds of children march past the visitors, led by their house captains. Each child wears his or her own special house color. After all the events of the day have been played, the houses have a tug of war until the strongest team has defeated the other two.

During their school years, boys and girls play the same types of sports. Later, girls might enjoy playing volleyball or swimming at a private, women's community center. A few may become professional table-tennis players and tour countries such as China to play in tournaments. Other sports are usually played only by men, but watched by both men and women.

Cricket and Kabaddi

Pakistanis are enthusiastic sports fans. Their favorite sports are cricket, field hockey, and squash, and their players are considered to be among the best in the world. Together, the whole Pakistani family watches sporting events.

On most afternoons, school grounds and parks, fields, and open areas in the cities are filled with cricket players of all ages. Cricket is a game similar to baseball, in which players try to score runs against an opposing team. In cricket, however, there are only two bases, or "wickets." Young boys—and men—enjoy playing in their special cricket uniforms—a white shirt, trousers, a little white cap, gloves, and a pair of protective shields to cover the knees.

A cricket game or match can vary in length. Just as in baseball, the team that scores the most runs wins. Pakistan's national cricket team travels often and competes against countries such as India, Australia, Great Britain, and the West Indies. Many Pakistani cricketers are known around the world. Retired cricketer Hanif Mohammed, in particular, holds two world records.

Whenever a professional cricket match is being played, fans throughout Pakistan listen to the match on radio, or follow it on live television. Taxi, rickshaw, and bus drivers turn on the radio quite loud so all their passengers can hear.

Pakistan is also well known for its field hockey players. Field hockey is similar to ice hockey, but it is played on a grass field. For many years, Pakistan has been among the best in this sport. In the 1960 and 1968 Olympic Games, Pakistan won the gold medal, and it has long been the field-hockey champion in the Asian Games. Almost all sports-loving Pakistanis are hockey fans. The game is so popular with young people that many schools have formed field hockey teams for girls.

Another favorite sport in Pakistan is squash. Squash

is an indoor game played on a small court with racquets. Similar to racquetball, it can be played with two or four players. Hashim Khan, a Pakistani, won seven world championships in squash within eight years. Khan wrote a book about the game of squash which has become a standard guide for squash players in many countries.

The Khan family is well known for its love of squash, and for its excellent players. Jehangir Khan, now in his early twenties, began playing squash when he was ten years old and became a professional at the age of sixteen. He has won the world squash championship three years in a row. Jehangir Khan travels year-round, playing in international tournaments and matches.

The British brought cricket, field hockey, tennis, and squash to the subcontinent, but the sixteenth-century Moghul king, Akbar, made polo popular. Polo is a team sport played on horseback. Members of each team race down a long field and attempt to use their mallets to hit a ball into the defender's goal. Pakistan holds many national polo competitions, especially during the annual horse and cattle shows in the provinces.

Another ancient Pakistani sport is *kabaddi*, a game of group wrestling. A player crosses into "enemy" territory and attempts to "kill" members of the other team by touching any one of them. But the player can only stay in the enemy field as long as he can repeat the

Jehangir Khan, champion squash player.

word "kabaddi" in the span of one deep breath! If the "enemy" team strikes and holds him until he runs out of breath, he is "killed" and his team loses him. Kabaddi is a fast game of endurance involving running, wrestling, and, of course, long, deep breathing!

Pakistani children play sports mainly at school. Most schools have several large playgrounds for their students. In the meantime, the younger children make the most of the open areas of the neighborhood. They fly their kites, play kabaddi, cricket, or hockey, or just run around playing tag. The government realizes that more sports and recreational centers should be provided for the country's youth, and has begun building sports centers in some areas of the country. Children of poor families do not have the money or equipment to train for professional sports. In the future, however, as more sports centers are built, Pakistanis hope the world will be seeing more of their athletes.

9. *Pakistanis in the United States*

For several decades, Pakistanis have been coming to the United States. Some leave their country to study in American colleges and universities. Many others, however, have decided to make the United States their home. They hope to have better opportunities than they would have had in Pakistan.

Today, almost 200,000 Pakistanis have become residents of the United States. Most live in and around big cities such as New York, Chicago, Houston, Washington, D.C., San Francisco, and Miami. Many of these Pakistanis are professionals who earn good salaries in the United States, and have a high standard of living here. In addition, about 45,000 Pakistanis live in Canada. Most of these people have professional jobs requiring technical or executive skills.

Although Pakistan's educational system has improved in past years, young Pakistanis are still attracted to the idea of studying and living in other countries, especially in North America. Wages are still very low in Pakistan. Some educated Pakistanis hope to work abroad, where they are highly paid for their skills.

Many Pakistanis who want to leave Pakistan wish to live in the United States. They have heard that working conditions are better, and that most employers pay good wages and treat their employees fairly. Pakistanis are willing to work hard to support their families.

Pakistani-American Families

When Pakistanis become American citizens, they are very proud of their new home. They may adapt to some American ways, yet they try to maintain the values taught by the Islamic religion. Schoolchildren, for example, may eat school lunches, but are careful not to eat any meat that is forbidden. A teenage Pakistani girl in the United States will not be seen in shorts or sundresses. She will not swim in a pool if people of both sexes are present.

Pakistani young people do not date and rarely attend parties because Islam does not allow men and women to dance together. Pakistani-American parents try to judge which social events will be suitable for their families, but it is not always easy. If they do attend parties, they will usually ask for soft drinks instead of liquor. At office parties, Pakistani Americans may leave soon after dinner, before the dancing begins.

Pakistani families in the United States often share their homes with relatives. Sometimes it is for a short period of time, to help newly arrived relatives settle in the city. But a young relative who is attending a university in the area may stay as a house guest for several years. When the parents of Pakistani-American families retire, they sometimes come to the United States to live with their children.

While these grandparents are impressed with how much the United States has to offer, they are sometimes shocked by American ways of life. They often remind their children and grandchildren not to waste water, electricity, or food, and to think about the less fortunate people in their homeland. Items such as dishwashers, microwave ovens, food processors, and vacuum cleaners can be a new experience for a Pakistani. In Pakistan, these products are very expensive, and even wealthy people go without them. Another example is newspapers. Pakistani newspapers are very small, and are always sold to vendors to be recycled. Imagine a Pakistani seeing an American newspaper on a Sunday!

Although many things change when Pakistanis move to the United States, the duties of a Pakistani-American homemaker remain much the same. The main responsibility of taking care of the house is still the woman's. Women do most of the housework and cooking, and care for the children. Men may help with most of the chores outside the house and sometimes care for the children. If families can afford to live on one salary, most Pakistani-American women stay home instead of pursuing a career.

Some Pakistani-American young people travel to Pakistan to learn more about their heritage. Here, a young man shows the fish he has caught with the help of a local tribesman.

Pakistani-American parents try to spend as much time with their families as possible so that the tradition of a close-knit family continues. Because American children have so much freedom, Pakistani-American parents feel their children need even more guidance. The young people may feel that their parents are being too strict or too protective. However, those boys and girls rarely argue with their parents or challenge their rules, because their religion frowns upon such behavior.

Most Pakistani-American teenagers do not move out of their parents' house until they get married. Even in this country, marriages are often still arranged, sometimes with a person living in Pakistan. However, many Pakistani Americans have an American spouse.

The Pakistani-American Community

Despite the fast-paced life in many American cities, Pakistani Americans still make time for their friends, and often invite each other for dinner on weekends. They look forward to celebrating holidays with each other, whether these holidays are American or Pakistani.

Pakistani Americans in major American and Canadian cities have formed local organizations to preserve their religion and heritage. Larger groups may rent a community hall for religious and social gatherings. The hall is always partitioned to accommodate men and women in separate sections.

In cities where the Pakistani-American community is not as large, the group of families meets at one person's home to celebrate events. Men and women sit in separate areas of the house. In many cities, Pakistani-American organizations have collected enough money to build their own community center or mosque. Muslims from countries other than Pakistan are also welcome to visit these mosques.

At a cultural show in Toronto, Pakistani folk dancers take part in a traditional dance.

During evenings in the month of Ramadhan, families bring homemade food to the center or mosque and break their fast together. On the morning of Eid-ul-Fitr or Eid-ul-Azha, the congregation recites Eid Namaaz in a group. A Pakistani restaurant or caterer cooks a meal for the whole community. After a traditional wedding ceremony is held at the mosque, many Pakistanis like to plan an elaborate wedding dinner at a local hotel the next day. At these formal dinners, men and women are not required to sit in separate sections, but may dine together with their families and friends.

On Sundays, the children of Pakistani-American parents may gather at a cultural center or in classrooms at a local school. Here, they learn Urdu, principles of the Islamic religion, and how to recite the Koran in Arabic. Most Pakistani-American children are bilingual, speaking English at school and Urdu at home. Though parents may be busy during the week, many of them volunteer their free time on weekends to teach at these schools.

Working in the United States

Many Pakistani Americans are professionals, employed in hospitals, laboratories, banks, law firms, universities, restaurants, or retail stores. In addition, many business-minded Pakistanis have become successful businesspeople. In most major American cities, Pakistani restaurants can be found. These restaurants may offer kebabs, tandoori chicken, curry, and many other traditional foods.

Other Pakistani-American shops offer printing services, dry cleaning, imported Pakistani handicrafts, garments, oriental and Pakistani rugs, and other items. Some Pakistanis have opened grocery stores, where they sell imported Pakistani spices, incense, rice, lentils, desserts, and fresh halaal meat. They may also rent the latest American, Indian, and Pakistani videocassettes. In larger cities, locally published newsletters in Urdu and English are popular, too. The newsletters report the latest news from Pakistan. They also carry advertisements of local Pakistani-American businesses and inform the community of upcoming events, such as the performances of Pakistani entertainers or musical groups that are touring North America.

While Pakistani Americans benefit from all that the United States has to offer, they also make a contribution to American society through their professions. Many Pakistani Americans play professional roles in science, business, education, and other fields.

Dr. Khalid Mahmood Butt of Brooklyn, New York, is one of the world's best surgeons specializing in kidney transplants. As the Director of the Down State Medical Center in Brooklyn, New York, Dr. Butt headed the world's ten biggest kidney transplant centers for eighteen years. During that time, this talented doctor and his team performed about two thousand kidney transplants. Butt, his wife, and two daughters live in New York, and his older daughter hopes to follow in her father's footsteps.

Other Pakistani Americans work for the United States government, and some work for the United Nations. Dr. Nafis Sadik is actively involved in the United

Dr. Khalid Butt.

Dr. Nafis Sadik.

Nations as the Executive Director of the United Nations Fund for Population Activity (UNFPA). Dr. Sadik holds the rank of Under-Secretary-General. She is one of the first women to head a major program at the United Nations. Dr. Sadik directs a worldwide staff of more than five hundred people. Before joining the United Nations in 1971, she practiced medicine in various Pakistani armed forces hospital for about ten years. Dr. Sadik and her husband have five children, two of whom are adopted.

With every passing year, more Pakistanis immigrate to the United States. They pass on stories of their homeland, its people, and its customs. As Americans learn more about Pakistan, Pakistanis hope that interest in and respect for their struggling young country will grow.

Appendix

Pakistani Embassies and Consulates in the United States and Canada

The Pakistani consulates in the United States and Canada offer assistance and information about Pakistani life. For information and resource materials about Pakistan, contact the embassy or consulate nearest you.

U.S. Consulates and Embassy

Boston, Massachusetts
Consulate General of Pakistan
745 Boylston Street
Boston, Massachusetts 02116
Phone (617) 267-9000

Chicago, Illinois
Consulate General of Pakistan
Suite 4700
One First National Plaza
Chicago, Illinois 60603
Phone (312) 853-7630

Houston, Texas
Consulate General of Pakistan
5555 Del Monte
Houston, Texas 77056
Phone (713) 963-9110

Louisville, Kentucky
Consulate General of Pakistan
1313 Abbeywood Road
Louisville, Kentucky 40222
Phone (502) 425-6053

New York, New York
Consulate General of Pakistan
12 East 65th Street
New York, New York 10021
Phone (212) 879-5800

San Francisco, California
Consulate General of Pakistan
211 Sutter Street
San Francisco, California 94108
Phone (415) 788-0677

Washington, D.C.
Embassy of Pakistan
2315 Massachusetts Avenue, N.W.
Washington, D.C. 20008
Phone (202) 939-6200

Canadian Consulates and Embassy

Montreal, Quebec
Consulate General of Pakistan
3421 Peel Street
Montreal, Quebec H3A 1W7
Phone (514) 845-2297

Ottawa, Ontario
Embassy of Pakistan
Burnside Building
151 Slater Street, Suite 608
Ottawa, Ontario K1P 5H3
Phone (613) 238-7881

Toronto, Ontario
Consulate General of Pakistan
4881 Yonge Street, Suite 810
Toronto, Ontario M2N 5X2
Phone (416) 250-1255

Glossary

Allah (AH·lah)—the Muslim name for God

Al-hamdu-lillah (ahl·HUHM·doo·lih·LAH)—an Arabic saying meaning, "praise to Allah"

ammi (uh·MEE)—mother

aqeeqa (ah·KEE·kuh)—a ceremony in which a newborn baby's hair is shaved off

Aryan (AIR·ee·uhn)—a group of people who invaded the Indian subcontinent in the 16th century

Ashura (ah·SHOOR·uh)—a day of mourning held on the tenth day of the Islamic month of Muharram

Assalaamo Alaikum (ah·SAH·lah·muh AH·lay·kum)—Arabic words of greeting, meaning "peace be upon you"

Awami Mela (ah·WAH·mih MAY·lah)—"People's Festival"; a six-day agricultural festival

azaan (ah·ZAHN)—a call for prayer announced from the minarets of mosques five times a day

bazaar (buh·ZAHR)—a busy marketplace

Bismillah (bihs·mihl·AH)—an Arabic phrase meaning, "In the name of Allah"

Bismillah ceremony—a ceremony in which a child learns the first Arabic alphabets of the Koran

Bismillahi-r-rahmaani-r-raheem (bihs·mihl·AH·ee·RAH·mah·nee·rah·HEEM)—an Arabic phrase meaning, "In the name of Allah the most compassionate and merciful"

bungalow (BUHN·gah·loh)—a house or villa owned by wealthier Pakistani families

chanda mama (chuhn·DAH mah·mah)—the legendary "uncle" on the moon

chapandoz (chuh·pahn·DOZ)—a polo-like game played by men on horseback

chappati (chuh·PAH·tee)—a flat bread, similar to a pancake; also known as roti

charpie (CHAHR·pee)—a four-legged wooden cot woven with ropes

dabbe-wallah (da·BEH·wah·lah)—a man who buys and sells boxes

dhobi wallah (DOH·bee·wah·lah)—a man who washes clothes for a living.

Dravidian (drah·VIH·dee·yan)—a group of people who once lived on the Indian subcontinent

dupatta (doo·PAH·tah)—a long scarf that Pakistani women drape over their chest and shoulders

Eid Mubarak (EED MU·bah·rahk)—a greeting exchanged on any Eid festival

Eid-ul-Azha (EED·ool·AH·zuh)—the Feast of the Sacrifice; a holiday celebrated during pilgrimage time

Eid-ul-Fitr (EED·ool·fee·trah)—the Feast of the Breaking of the Fast; celebrated after the month of Ramadhan

ghazal (GUH·zuhl)—a slow, melodious Pakistani song set to the words of a poem

Hadith (hah·DEES)—the sayings of the Prophet Muhammad

Hajj (HAJ)—a pilgrimage that every Muslim must take once in his or her lifetime to the holy city of Mecca

Hajjis (HAH·jeez)—titles of honor given to Muslims who have been on the Hajj pilgrimage

halaal (huh·LAH·ahl)—according to Islam, anything that is allowed or honestly possessed

haraam (huh·RAH·ahm)—according to Islam, anything that is not allowed or dishonestly possessed)

hookah (HOO·kuh)—a long smoking pipe shared by several people

iftaar (ihf·TAHR)—the breaking of a fast at dusk

inshaallah (ihn·shah·LAH)—an Arabic phrase meaning, "If Allah wills"

Islam (ihs·LAHM)—a religion whose followers pray to, and believe in only one God, Allah

Juma (joo·MAH)—Friday; the Muslim sabbath

kabaddi (kuh·BAH·dee)—a game of tag

kasida (kuh·SEE·dah)—a poem sung in praise of Prophet Muhammad

Koran (kohr·AHN)—the holy book of Islam revealed to Prophet Muhammad by Allah

mehndi (MAYN·dee)—henna paste applied on the hands and feet of brides, or on the hands of children during certain Eid celebrations

Muharram (muh·huh·RAHM)—the first month in the

Islamic calendar; also a month of mourning

Muslim (MUS·lihm)—a follower of Islam

naagan (nah·GAN)—a snake that, according to legend, can take the form of a forest maiden

namaaz (nah·MAHZ)—prayers said by a Muslim five times a day

nikah (nih·KAH)—the recitation of a wedding "contract" between a Muslim man and woman

purdah (PUHR·duh)—a covering of the head and body, except for the face, hands, and feet, worn by Muslim women

qazi (KAH·zee)—a Muslim religious scholar who can recite nikah

Qissa Khawani (KISS·ah Kah·WAH·nee)—street of story-tellers

Ramadhan (rah·man·DAHN)—the Muslim month of fasting

roti (ROH·tee)—a flat, unleavened round bread

shalwar kamiz (SHAHL·wahr kah·MEEZ)—a long, knee-length shirt and baggy pants worn by Pakistani men and women; women usually wear a dupatta with the outfit

sitar (sih·TAHR)—a large, stringed musical instrument

tabla (TAHB·lah)—a pair of drums

tandoor (tuhn·DOOR)—an extremely hot oven buried deep below ground

Selected Bibliography

Amin, Mohammed, and Duncan Willetts. *Journey Through Pakistan*. London, England: Bodley Head, 1982.

Amin, Mohammed. *We Live in Pakistan*. New York, New York: The Bookwright Press, 1985

Burki, Shahid Javed. *Pakistan: A Nation in the Making*. Boulder, Colorado: Westview Press, 1986.

Caldwell, John C. *Let's Visit Pakistan*. Connecticut: Burke Publishing Co., Ltd., 1983.

Collins, Larry, and Dominique Lapierre. *Freedom at Midnight*. New York, New York: Simon & Schuster, 1975.

Government Printing Office. *Pakistan: A Country Study*. Washington, D.C., 1984.

Reeves, Richard. *Passage to Peshawar*. New York, New York: Simon & Schuster, 1984.

Santiago, Jose Roleo. *Pakistan: A Travel Survival Kit*. Oakland, California: Lonely Planet Publications, 1987.

Theroux, Paul. *The Imperial Way*. Boston, Massachusetts: Houghton Mifflin, Inc., 1985.

Index

About the Author

Jabeen Yusufali has traveled extensively throughout Pakistan as both resident and visitor. In addition to educating American children about Pakistan, she believes it is important for Pakistani-American children to learn more about their heritage.

Ms. Yusufali is a freelance writer, and has published a number of articles for children. She lives with her husband and two children in Minnesota.